American Biographies

AMELIA EARHART

Robin S. Doak

Heinemann
LIBRARY

Chicago, Illinois

www.capstonepub.com
Visit our website to find out more information about Heinemann-Raintree books.

To order:
☎ Phone 888-454-2279
▣ Visit www.capstonepub.com
to browse our catalog and order online.

Edited by Abby Colich, Megan Cotugno, and Laura Hensley
Designed by Cynthia Della-Rovere
Original illustrations © Capstone Global Library
  Limited 2011
Illustrated by Oxford Designers & Illustrators
Picture research by Tracy Cummins
Originated by Capstone Global Library Limited
Printed and bound in China by Leo Paper Group

16 15 14 13 12
10 9 8 7 6 5 4 3 2 1

Library of Congress Cataloging-in-Publication Data
Doak, Robin S. (Robin Santos), 1963-
  Amelia Earhart / Robin S. Doak.
    p. cm.—(American biographies)
  Includes bibliographical references and index.
  ISBN 978-1-4329-6451-1 (hb)—ISBN 978-1-4329-6462-7 (pb) 1. Earhart, Amelia, 1897-1937—Juvenile literature. 2. Air pilots—United States—Biography—Juvenile literature. 3. Women air pilots—United States—Biography—Juvenile literature. I. Title.
  TL540.E3D63 2013
  629.13092—dc23   2011037575
  [B]

Acknowledgments
The author and publishers are grateful to the following for permission to reproduce copyright material: AP Photo: p. 30; Corbis: pp. 6 (© Bettmann), 8 (© Underwood & Underwood), 16 (© Bettmann), 17 (© Bettmann), 21 (© CORBIS), 23 (© Underwood & Underwood), 25 (© Bettmann), 27 (© Underwood & Underwood), 29 (© Bettmann), 33 (© CORBIS), 34 (© Bettmann), 35 (© Bettmann), 37 (© Bettmann); Getty Images: pp. 7, 19 (Central Press/Hulton Archive), 20 (New York Times Co), 28 (Topical Press Agency), 38 (NY Daily News), 39 (Time & Life Pictures), 40 (AFP); Library of Congress Prints and Photographs: pp. 12, 15; NASA: p. 5 (Smithsonian Institution); Newscom: p. 9 (ZUMA Press); Purdue University Libraries, Karnes Archives and Special Collections: pp. 11, 24, 31).

Cover photograph of Aviatrix Amelia Earhart in cockpit of plane on December 15, 1930, reproduced with permission from Getty Images (Time & Life Pictures).

Every effort has been made to contact copyright holders of material reproduced in this book. Any omissions will be rectified in subsequent printings if notice is given to the publisher.

Contents

Some words are shown in bold, **like this**.
These words are explained in the glossary.

More Than a Pilot

During her lifetime Amelia Earhart was one of the most famous women in the world. Best known as a **pioneer** in the newborn **aviation** industry, Earhart was also an author, speaker, **social worker**, and counselor. She set many flight records and—at a time when women were discouraged from flying—proved that women could fly as well as men. She also helped found some of the first **commercial** airlines.

Earhart was the perfect representative for women in aviation. Her honest, straightforward manner won her friends and admirers everywhere she went. Her bold and fearless nature allowed her to take chances that others were afraid to take.

Earhart was a strong supporter of women's rights. At a time when aviation and other industries were dominated by men, Earhart showed that women could do whatever they chose. She hoped that her example would encourage other women to try new things and achieve greatness.

Fact VS. Fiction

Myth: Amelia Earhart was an incompetent pilot who should never have attempted a round-the-world flight.

Fact: Earhart logged many hours in the air and set several flight records. She may not have been the most skilled or talented female flyer of her time, but she was a competent pilot who could handle the hard-to-fly airplanes of the 1920s and 1930s.

Despite all of her accomplishments, Earhart became a legend because of her final failure. Her disappearance over the Pacific Ocean on July 2, 1937, remains one of aviation's greatest mysteries. Today people still wonder what, exactly, became of the famous flyer.

Amelia Earhart disappeared shortly before her 40th birthday.

Young Amelia

Amelia Mary Earhart was born in Atchison, Kansas, on July 24, 1897. Her father, Edwin Earhart, was a lawyer for the railroads. Her mother, Amy Otis Earhart, was a housewife. Amelia had one younger sister, Grace Muriel, born in 1899. The two would remain close throughout Amelia's life.

Edwin's job required him to be frequently on the move. So until she was 11, Amelia lived with her grandparents, Alfred and Amelia Otis, for most of the year. The Otises put a high value on education and learning. Amelia loved to read, and she was a good student.

Amelia and her sister moved to Des Moines, Iowa, when Amelia was in the seventh grade.

Amelia was a tomboy who often came home with skinned knees and bruises from climbing up trees and onto rooftops.

Amelia was also a **tomboy**. She played basketball, baseball, tennis, and football. She swam, fished, and rode horses. Amelia's mother encouraged her girls to be active. She even sewed **bloomers** for them to wear—although girls of this time only wore skirts.

When Amelia was 10, she and her family visited the Iowa State Fair. Here she saw her first airplane. Amelia was not impressed. She later wrote, "It was a thing of rusty wire and wood and looked not at all interesting."

Did you know?

Amelia, her sister, and two playmates built a roller coaster in her grandparents' backyard. The Earhart girls had seen a roller coaster at the 1904 St. Louis **World's Fair** but had been forbidden to ride it.

Moving around

Amelia's later childhood was more unsettled. Although the Earhart family was together again, Edwin Earhart began drinking a lot of alcohol. He moved from job to job, and the family struggled to pay their bills. In 1915 Amy left her husband and moved with the two girls to Chicago, Illinois.

Young Amelia was independent. Her high school yearbook photograph was captioned: "A.E.—the girl in brown who walks alone."

Did you know?

The first woman recorded taking flight was Frenchwoman Elisabeth Thible in 1784. Thible was a passenger in a hot-air balloon.

Amelia worked long, hard hours as a nurse's aide in Toronto, Canada.

In 1915 Amelia graduated from a Chicago high school and moved to Pennsylvania to attend a junior college. During Christmas break the following year, Amelia visited Muriel in Toronto, Canada. There she saw Canadian soldiers who had been seriously wounded while fighting in **World War I**. Although Amelia was just months from graduating, she decided to stay in Canada and help. She worked as a nurse's aide, scrubbing floors, handing out medicines, and serving meals.

In Toronto, Amelia became fascinated by airplanes and flight. She visited some of her old patients at airfields around the city. She later wrote that one of the little red planes "said something to me as it swished by."

In early 1919 Amelia moved to New York City to attend Columbia University. She left at the end of her first year to live with her parents, who had reunited and were living in Los Angeles, California.

First flight

In 1920 Earhart took her first flight in an airplane. Edwin Earhart paid a pilot in Los Angeles $10 so that Earhart could have a 10-minute plane ride. She later wrote, "As soon as we left the ground, I knew I myself had to fly."

At this time **aviation** was still in its early years. The Wright brothers had made the first successful airplane flight in 1903, yet planes were still uncomfortable and difficult to handle. Pilots couldn't fly at night because few flight instruments existed, and there were no laws governing air flight. Most Americans distrusted this new form of travel.

Because of the danger involved, Earhart's parents disapproved of her desire to fly. But they eventually gave in to letting her learn, on one condition: Earhart must learn with a female flight instructor. Although aviation was almost completely dominated by men, Earhart found female pilot Neta Snook (see box). She trained with Neta for a year before flying alone.

Mary Anita "Neta" Snook

(1896–1991)

Growing up in Iowa, Neta Snook became fascinated by automobiles. Her father taught her to be a capable **mechanic**. As airplanes became popular, Snook decided that she wanted to learn how to fly. But when she applied to a flight school in Virginia, her application was rejected with the words "No females allowed." Snook persisted and eventually became the first woman to own her own flying school and run a **commercial** airfield.

Earhart's first airplane, purchased in 1921, was a two-seat, bright yellow **biplane** that she called the Canary.

Learning to Soar

Earhart quickly realized that what she wanted most in life was to fly. During the week she worked as a telephone operator and performed other odd jobs in order to raise money and continue flying. On weekends she headed to the airfield, climbed into her plane, and soared into the sky.

During the 1920s, many pilots earned money at air shows by performing flying stunts and taking passengers for short rides.

On October 22, 1922, Earhart set her first flight record at Rogers Field in California. Piloting the *Canary*, she climbed to an **altitude** of 14,000 feet (4,300 meters). This was an unofficial women's record for the highest flight. Five months later, Earhart appeared as a **stunt flyer** at an air rodeo in Glendale, California. In the *Canary*, Earhart performed loops, spins, and rolls.

Earhart quickly learned that not everyone supported her flying. At this time, many male pilots were openly hostile to women pilots. They believed that women should not be piloting airplanes at all. Some female flyers even had their planes **sabotaged** by men who wanted to make sure the women kept their feet on the ground.

Did you know?

When she was learning to fly, Earhart began cutting her long, blond hair, an inch at a time, so her mother wouldn't notice. She also began wearing pants and other "masculine" clothing.

Helping others

In 1924 Earhart's parents divorced. Earhart sold her plane, bought a car, and drove back to the East Coast to be near her sister, Muriel, who now lived in Massachusetts. It would be five years before Earhart owned another airplane.

In Massachusetts, Earhart found work as a tutor, teaching English to foreign students. In the fall of 1926, she took a job as a **social worker** at Denison House, a Boston-area **settlement house**. A settlement house is a community center in a poor neighborhood that provides many types of services. Here Earhart taught English and worked with children.

In 1927 she began flying on weekends again, piloting borrowed planes. Earhart's flights brought her attention from the press, and she used the attention to advance herself and other women as well. One article described her as "very much a **feminist**."

Charles Lindbergh

(1902–1974)

When U.S. pilot Charles Lindbergh touched down in Paris, France, he became the first person to cross the Atlantic Ocean in an airplane. The trip, which lasted more than 33 hours, made "Lucky Lindy" an international hero. Lindbergh was honored by President Calvin Coolidge and celebrated with a huge **ticker tape parade** in New York City. Today, Lindbergh's plane, the *Spirit of St. Louis*, can be seen at the National Air and Space Museum in Washington, D.C.

In 1927 Charles Lindbergh's historic trans-Atlantic flight in the *Spirit of St. Louis* created excitement and interest in **aviation**. Earhart was one of those people thrilled and inspired by the flight.

Getting Serious

In April 1928, Earhart was working at Denison House when she received an important phone call. A group of pilots was looking for a woman to be the first female passenger to cross the Atlantic Ocean by plane. Was she interested?

Earhart was extremely interested. She traveled to New York to interview with the flight's organizers. One of men she met with was publisher George P. Putnam. G. P., as he was known, would come to play an important role in Earhart's life.

Up front, the men warned her that the trip could be dangerous. Already, three women had died trying to follow in Lucky Lindy's footsteps. A news article written after one of the failures summed up how most people felt about a woman making the crossing: "Men…may strive to equal Lindbergh. Women should stay home." But Earhart was ready to prove that women belonged in the air.

Earhart was assigned the role of commander on the flight. Bill Stultz, shown here, was the pilot, and Slim Gordon served as mechanic.

Earhart's physical resemblance to Charles Lindbergh—as well as her flying feats—earned her the nickname Lady Lindy.

Wilmer "Bill" Stultz

(1899–1929)

At the age of 29, Bill Stultz was already an experienced flyer. He had served in the Army Air Force and the Naval Air Service. During his time in the military, he received special **aviation** training. Stultz was also a flight trainer, **test pilot**, and winner of a national air speed race. His career ended abruptly in 1929, when he was killed during a **test flight**.

Preparing for adventure

Earhart was excited to begin her adventure, but she prepared for the worst. She wrote up a **will** and penned letters to her parents. The letters were to be delivered if she did not return from the flight. The one to her father read, "Hooray for the last grand adventure!"

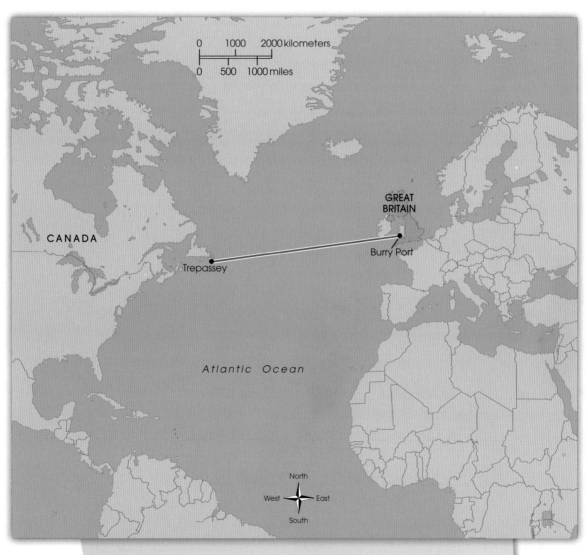

The flight path of the *Friendship* carried the crew nearly 2,000 miles (3,200 kilometers) from Canada to Wales.

When the *Friendship* landed in Wales, Earhart instantly became famous—even though she described herself as "just baggage, like a sack of potatoes."

On June 4 Earhart, pilot Bill Stultz, and mechanic Louis "Slim" Gordon arrived in Trepassey, a town in Newfoundland, Canada. The three flew in the *Friendship*, the plane that would be used to make the Atlantic crossing. The *Friendship* had been equipped with a **state-of-the-art** compass, as well as two radios.

The airplane had also been specially fitted with **pontoons** that would keep it afloat if it crashed into the Atlantic Ocean. However, the pontoons also meant that the plane could only take off from and land in water. The crew of the *Friendship* spent 13 days in Trepassey waiting for the right weather conditions. But even when the weather was good, the heavy plane could not lift out of the water.

On June 17, just before noon, the plane finally took flight. Slim Gordon had been forced to toss out all of their extra fuel to make the plane light enough to take off. But at long last, the three were headed toward the United Kingdom.

Making history

Throughout the long trip, Earhart took notes in her journal. She recorded the plane's progress and any comments made by her crewmates, as well as her own thoughts and feelings. She wrote about the heavy fog and fierce storm the crew flew through. She also made a note when the plane's radio stopped working.

After nearly 21 hours in the air, the plane landed on some water near Burry Port, Wales. Although no one was there to greet them, word soon spread that the plane had landed. Within hours hundreds of people gathered on the shore. They were all there to see Amelia Earhart, the first woman to cross the Atlantic Ocean in a plane.

Earhart was amazed by the greeting she received in Wales.

Earhart received a ticker tape parade in New York after her flight across the Atlantic.

It was now Earhart's turn to become famous around the world. Newspapers covered her story, and everyone wanted to meet her. In London she was invited to dinners, parties, and other events in her honor. The crew of the *Friendship* returned to New York City on July 6 by ship. They took part in a **ticker tape parade**, driving to City Hall in an open car. Thousands lined Broadway to get a good look at Earhart.

Did you know?

After her successful trip, *Cosmopolitan* magazine hired Earhart as its aviation editor. Earhart wrote articles titled, "Shall You Let Your Daughter Fly?" and "Why Are Women Afraid to Fly?"

Suddenly famous

After the *Friendship* flight, Earhart devoted her life to flying. G. P. Putnam began managing her career, making sure that she was always in the public eye. He scheduled her to appear at public benefits, at lectures, and with Hollywood celebrities. Those who met her found Earhart entertaining, down-to-earth, and likable.

Putnam also secured jobs for Earhart endorsing products, and soon she was appearing in newspaper and magazine advertisements around the country. Putnam also made sure that photographers were on hand when Earhart appeared in public. Americans grew to recognize her trademark short, curly, blond hair and her favorite flying outfit: knee-high leather boots, leather jacket, and flying **goggles**.

Soon after coming home, Earhart used her journals to write a book about the historic crossing of the Atlantic Ocean. She called the book *20 Hrs., 40 Min.*, which was the amount of time that it had taken for the *Friendship* to cross the Atlantic. Earhart wrote the book while staying with Putnam and his wife at their home in Rye, New York.

Although she was busy, Earhart flew as much as she could. She had bought a new, open-**cockpit** plane in London, and she wanted to use it. In September 1928, Earhart made a cross-country trip from New York to California. When she returned to the East Coast in October, she set a record for the first female solo flight from the Atlantic to the Pacific and back again.

Earhart stayed quite busy endorsing products, writing her book, and flying as often as possible.

Reaching New Heights

Earhart remained very busy during 1929 and 1930. In March 1929, she passed a four-hour written exam, physical, and flight test to receive a U.S. Department of Commerce transport pilot's license. She was only the fourth woman to receive the license.

In July 1929, Earhart was appointed to a position at Transcontinental Air Transport, a new airline. A year later, she was appointed vice president of another new airline, called the Ludington Line. The Ludington flew routes that connected Washington, D.C., Philadelphia, and New York.

Earhart, shown at the far left, was one of the first passengers on the newly formed Transcontinental Air Transport.

Earhart, shown here waving a flag, competed against other women pilots many times.

In August 1929, Earhart, along with 19 other pilots, took part in the first Women's Air Derby, nicknamed the Powder Puff Derby. This cross-country air race began in Santa Monica, California, and ended in Cleveland, Ohio.

After the race, Earhart and some of the other women got together to talk about starting a group for female pilots. The group was called the Ninety-Nines, for the number of original members. The first meeting of the Ninety-Nines took place in November 1929 in Long Island, New York. The group continues to meet to this day.

Despite her accomplishments, critics and some fellow pilots pointed out Earhart's weaknesses as a pilot. They pointed to small crashes, minor accidents, and emergency landings that she was involved in. Putnam made sure that most of these events were blamed on **mechanical** problems.

A partnership with G. P. Putnam

G. P. Putnam had been spending a lot of time with Earhart since the Atlantic crossing in 1928. He traveled with her, organized her schedule, set up speaking engagements, and even gave her advice on how to dress, talk, and stand. In late 1929, Putnam and his wife Dorothy divorced.

George P. Putnam
(1887–1950)

Early in his career, George P. Putnam worked for his family's publishing company in New York City. In 1927 he published Charles Lindbergh's autobiography, called *We*. After he met Earhart in 1928, Putnam devoted his efforts to promoting and publicizing her career as a pilot. After her disappearance, Putnam donated many of Earhart's documents and belongings to Purdue University (see page 31).

Putnam asked Earhart to marry him a number of times before she finally accepted. The young pilot was not eager to give up her independence. The two were finally married on February 7, 1931. After the wedding, she remained known as Amelia Earhart instead of Amelia Putnam. This was an unusual step at the time. She also chose to not wear a wedding ring.

Now that Earhart was making good money, she took care of her family. She paid off her father's debts and bought clothes for her mother. She also remained close to her sister Muriel, whom she called Pidge. Earhart helped Pidge and her husband buy a home in Massachusetts.

Earhart and Putnam both agreed to a marriage that was also a partnership.

This photo shows Earhart in the **cockpit** of her plane after her solo trans-Atlantic flight.

In Lindy's footsteps

By 1932 **aviation** had come a long way. New instruments made flying safer, and pilots were setting new flight records. In 1931, for example, pilot Wiley Post and his **navigator** flew around the world in just over eight days. Yet no one had successfully repeated Lindbergh's historic solo cross-Atlantic journey.

On May 20—the fifth anniversary of Lindbergh's historic flight—Earhart took off from an airport in Newfoundland, Canada. Her red and gold Lockheed Vega airplane had been specially prepared for the trip. All the seats had been removed so that she could carry extra fuel. **Mechanics** installed new instruments and a strong new engine on the little plane.

A crowd surrounds Earhart's plane after she becomes the first female to fly solo across the Atlantic.

The flight was not an easy one. During the course of the trip, Earhart flew through heavy fog and storms. She also dealt with icy wings, engine problems, and instruments that didn't work properly. At one point, the plane even dropped nearly 3,000 feet (900 meters) and went into a spin!

Earhart landed in Northern Ireland 15 hours and 18 minutes after she took flight. She had overcome all obstacles and succeeded where many others had failed. She had become the first woman—and the second pilot—to fly solo across the Atlantic Ocean.

Did you know?

Earhart was the first woman to test-fly an **autogiro**. This machine is a cross between an airplane and a helicopter.

Keeping busy

After her cross-Atlantic flight, Earhart was an international superstar, one of the most famous women in the world. But instead of slowing down and relaxing, Earhart became even busier. Soon after returning from Europe, she flew nonstop from Los Angeles to New York. It was the first such flight made by a woman pilot.

Did you know?

In 1934 Earhart founded a line of designer clothing that she called Amelia Earhart Fashions. The clothing was sold in department stores and included dresses, suits, hats, luggage, and other items. Each item included an aviation trademark—a parachute cord belt, for example, or a wing bolt as a button.

Earhart offered to teach First Lady Eleanor Roosevelt how to fly, but President Roosevelt said no to the idea.

In the coming years, Earhart set a number of new flight records. There were records for speed, distance, and new routes. Earhart also continued to travel throughout the country, giving speeches to packed crowds wherever she went. In 1933 she even found the time to help organize a third airline, Boston-Maine Airways. The little airline survived through the years and eventually became part of Delta.

In 1935 Earhart took a job at Purdue University in Indiana. Here she counseled young female students and taught courses in **aeronautics**. Purdue also bought a new plane for Earhart. She called the specially designed, multiengine plane her "flying laboratory." And she began to make plans for the biggest adventure of her life.

As a counselor at Purdue University, Earhart encouraged female students to pursue their dreams.

The Final Flight

In 1935 Earhart began planning a flight that would keep her in the spotlight. She wanted to be the first female to pilot an airplane around the world. She believed that, with her new plane, this 29,000-mile (46,000-kilometer) trip would be possible.

To prepare for the trip, Earhart spent hours flying in her new plane. After each flight the plane was altered and improved to prepare for the round-the-world attempt. By 1937 it was equipped with extra gas tanks as well as the latest in radio receivers, direction-finding instruments, and other gear.

Fact VS. Fiction

Myth: Earhart's male copilots performed the most difficult tasks.

Fact: In 1937 Earhart allowed copilot Paul Mantz to help her take off in Oakland and land in Honolulu. After newspapers reported that her male crew was doing all the work, she refused to allow the men to be in the **cockpit** during takeoff or landing again.

On March 17, 1937, Earhart and three male crew members took off from Oakland, California. Their proposed route would take them in a westward direction around the world. About 16 hours later, they arrived at their first stop in Honolulu, Hawaii.

Disaster struck on March 20 while Earhart was taking off from Honolulu. While moving down the runway, the right wing of the plane clipped the ground and the plane spun out of control. The landing gear collapsed, and the plane skidded along the runway. Although no one was hurt, the plane was badly damaged.

Earhart's crash in Honolulu halted her dreams to fly around the world.

Starting over

Soon after the crash in Honolulu, Earhart announced that she would fix the "flying laboratory" and try again. For the second trip, Earhart would fly eastward around the world. And she would take only one crew member with her, experienced **navigator** Fred Noonan (see box).

On May 20, 1937, Earhart took off from Oakland, California. The second round-the-world flight attempt had begun. After picking up Fred Noonan in Burbank, California, the pair headed east. They made stops in Tucson, Arizona, and New Orleans, Louisiana. On May 23 they landed in Miami, Florida, their last U.S. stop.

Earhart carefully selected the most important supplies for her last journey.

Over the next month, Earhart and Noonan covered hundreds of miles. They landed in Puerto Rico before setting out for South America, where they made four stops. From there it was on to Africa, Asia, and Australia. On June 29 they finally landed in Lae, a town on the island of New Guinea.

Fred Noonan

(1893–1937)

Fred Noonan was one of the most experienced navigators whom Earhart could have chosen. Noonan had learned his navigation skills at sea, first as a regular seaman and later as an officer during **World War I**. During a seven-year career as chief navigator with Pan American Airways, Noonan had **surveyed** the Pacific region for possible flight routes. He had also flown with Earhart on her first round-the-world attempt.

Gone without a trace

Although Earhart had completed nearly two-thirds of her trip, the most difficult part lay just ahead. The flight from Lae, New Guinea, to Howland Island had never been flown before. Earhart and Noonan would be the first to land on the tiny island in the middle of the Pacific Ocean. To help Earhart locate the island, the U.S. Coast Guard ship *Itasca* waited off its coast. It would send signals to guide the plane.

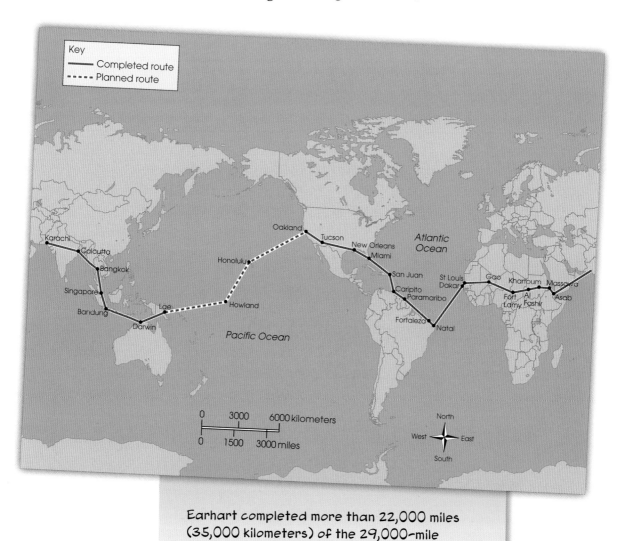

Earhart completed more than 22,000 miles (35,000 kilometers) of the 29,000-mile (46,000-kilometer) flight around the world.

At 10:00 a.m. on July 2, the "flying laboratory" took flight. A message was immediately sent to the *Itasca*, telling the ship to prepare for Earhart's arrival in about 18 hours. As the plane got closer to the island, the *Itasca* began receiving radio messages from Earhart. The signals got stronger and stronger, but Earhart didn't seem to hear any of the messages the *Itasca* sent in return.

More than 18 hours into the flight, Earhart broadcast the following message to the *Itasca*: "We must be on you but cannot see you. Gas is running low. Been unable to reach you by radio." Earhart and Noonan were unable to locate the small Pacific island.

An hour later the *Itasca* heard another message. This time the signal was weaker than it had been before. Earhart reported that she was still trying to find the island. It was the last time anyone heard from Amelia Earhart.

When Earhart and Noonan left New Guinea, they had just three stops left on their round-the-world trip.

The search begins

The search for Earhart and Noonan began. Dozens of ships and planes searched for thousands of miles around Howland Island—with no success. On July 18 all efforts were abandoned. The plane had disappeared without a trace. But the end of the search was just the beginning of the mystery.

Theories about Earhart's fate were put forth to explain the mystery. Some thought that Earhart and Noonan survived the crash, only to be taken prisoner by the Japanese. Others believed that Earhart landed the plane on one of the small islands near Howland Island. There she might have survived for months or years before dying.

What exactly happened to Earhart and Noonan? Many experts believe that the most likely explanation is the simplest: The two died when their plane crashed into the sea after running out of gas. The plane probably lies today on the ocean floor.

News of Earhart's disappearance shocked readers around the world.

DAILY NEWS FINAL

EARHART PLANE LOST AT SEA

Amelia Earhart Missing on World Flight

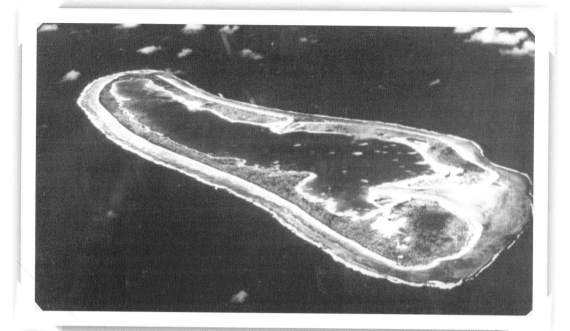

In 2007 researchers found a zipper, mirror, and buttons on an island near where Earhart's plane may have crashed. In 2010 they found tiny bone chips on the same island. There is no proof that the materials were Earhart's.

Fact VS. Fiction

Myth: Earhart lived out her life as a housewife in New Jersey.

Fact: This story began in 1965 when a researcher met an older woman at a luncheon in Long Island. The man became convinced that this woman, Irene Bolam, was in fact Amelia Earhart. A book with his theory was written in 1970, even though Mrs. Bolam denied being the lost flyer.

A Flying Legend

The mystery of Earhart's disappearance is still interesting today because it has never been solved. However, Earhart's true importance is in her contributions to **aviation** and women's rights. Earhart was a record setter and **pioneer**. She pushed the limits and showed that women were as capable as men—in flight and on the ground.

Earhart loved flying her plane.

Earhart contributed to the growth of aviation by testing new airplanes and learning about their strengths and weaknesses. She also made the American public—especially women—more confident in the safety of flying.

Earhart was also a successful businesswoman. She founded airlines and designed her own line of clothing. With her husband, she turned her own accomplishments and image into a brand and became famous around the world.

Earhart always understood the rewards and risks every time she got into the **cockpit**. In a note to her husband, written before one of her flights, Earhart wrote: "Please know I want to do it because I want to do it. Women must try to do things as men have tried. When they fail, their failure must be but a challenge to others."

Did you know?

Despite the strides made by Earhart and other female pilots of her day, only 6 percent of all licensed pilots in the United States today are women.

Timeline

1897

Amelia Earhart is born in Atchison, Kansas, on July 24.

1915

Earhart graduates from high school in Chicago.

1917

Earhart visits her sister, Muriel, in Toronto, Canada, and sees wounded World War I soldiers.

1918

While working in a Toronto military hospital, Earhart begins visiting military airfields and watching pilots fly.

1924

Earhart and her mother drive across the country to settle near Muriel in Massachusetts.

1921

In January Earhart begins flying lessons with Anita Snook. At the end of the year, Earhart receives her pilot's license and takes part in an air show.

1920

Earhart leaves Columbia University to go live with her parents in Los Angeles. In December she takes her first ride in a plane.

1925

Earhart takes a job in Boston teaching English to foreign students. Later in the year, she works at a hospital.

1926

Earhart is hired as a social worker at Denison House in Boston.

1928

Earhart becomes the first female passenger to make a cross-Atlantic flight on June 17–18. She writes *20 Hrs., 40 Min.*, a book about the trip.

1930

In September Earhart's father dies of stomach cancer.

1929

Earhart participates in the Powder Puff Derby, a cross-country air race for women. After the race is over, Earhart helps found the Ninety-Nines, a pilots' association for women.

1928

In September and October, Earhart makes the first round-trip, cross-country flight by a woman. In November she is named aviation editor at *Cosmopolitan* magazine.

1931

Earhart marries G. P. Putnam on February 7.

1932

In May Earhart becomes the first female pilot to make a solo flight across the Atlantic Ocean.

1934

Earhart founds her own line of designer clothing and luggage.

1935

Earhart accepts a position at Purdue University counseling female students. She also sets a number of flight records this year.

1939

On January 5, Earhart is declared dead by a judge in California.

1937

On May 20 Earhart begins her second attempt to fly around the world. On July 2 her plane disappears somewhere around Howland Island in the Pacific Ocean.

1936

Earhart is given the "flying laboratory," a brand-new plane that she will use to attempt a round-the-world flight.

Family Tree

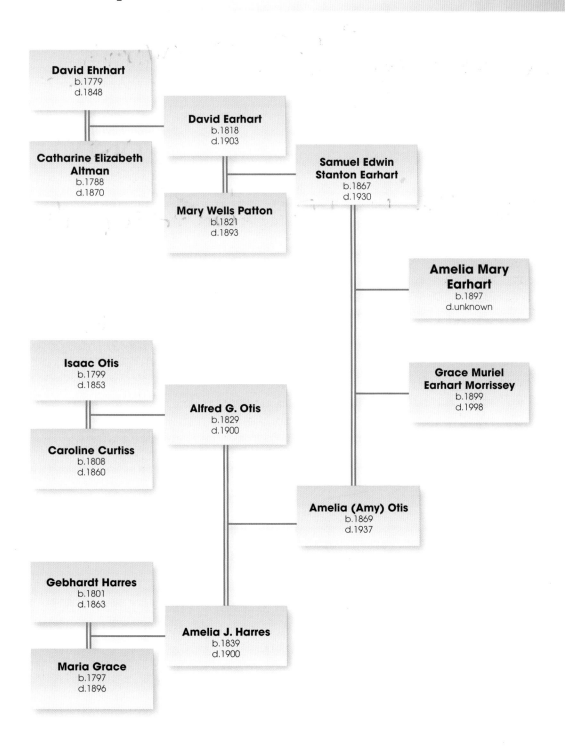

David Ehrhart
b.1779
d.1848

David Earhart
b.1818
d.1903

Catharine Elizabeth Altman
b.1788
d.1870

Samuel Edwin Stanton Earhart
b.1867
d.1930

Mary Wells Patton
b.1821
d.1893

Amelia Mary Earhart
b.1897
d.unknown

Isaac Otis
b.1799
d.1853

Alfred G. Otis
b.1829
d.1900

Grace Muriel Earhart Morrissey
b.1899
d.1998

Caroline Curtiss
b.1808
d.1860

Amelia (Amy) Otis
b.1869
d.1937

Gebhardt Harres
b.1801
d.1863

Amelia J. Harres
b.1839
d.1900

Maria Grace
b.1797
d.1896

Glossary

aeronautics
science of the design and making of aircraft

altitude
height above Earth's surface

autogiro
aircraft that has the features of both a helicopter and an airplane

aviation
science of flying and navigating airplanes

bloomers
loose pants that are gathered tightly at the ankle

cockpit
space where the pilot sits in an airplane

commercial
having to do with business or trade

feminist
someone who believes in equal rights for women

goggles
eyewear that protects the eyes from wind, dust, and other items

mechanic
worker who is skilled at repairing machines

mechanical
of or relating to machines

navigator
person who directs one's course in an aircraft, ship, or vehicle

pioneer
person who explores new areas

pontoon
floats on the bottom of a plane that allow it to land in the water

sabotage

to do intentional damage

settlement house

community center in a poor neighborhood that provides many types of services

social worker

someone who works to improve conditions in a neighborhood, school, or family

state of the art

most up-to-date technology available

stunt flyer

pilot who performs rolls and other tricks while flying

survey

to measure an area in order to determine its size and characteristics

test flight

flight to test new aircraft

test pilot

pilot who tests new airplanes

ticker tape parade

parade in which pieces of torn paper are thrown into the air

tomboy

girl who likes to take part in physical activities and play sports

will

document that details how a person's goods will be divided after he or she has died

World War I

war that took place from 1914 to 1918 and involved all the major powers in the world

World's Fair

large, public exhibitions that have been held periodically around the world since 1851

Find Out More

Books

Burleigh, Robert. *Night Flight: Amelia Earhart Crosses the Atlantic.* New York: Simon and Schuster Books for Young Readers, 2011.

Earhart, Amelia. *The Fun of It: Random Records of My Own Flying and of Women in Aviation.* Chicago: Academy Press, 1977.

Earhart, Amelia. *Last Flight: Amelia Earhart's Flying Adventures.* Coventry, U.K.: Trotamundas Press, 2008.

Nahum, Andrew. *Flight.* New York: Dorling Kindersley, 2011.

Reed, Jennifer. *Daring American Heroes of Flight: 9 Brave Fliers.* Berkeley Heights, N.J.: MyReportLinks.com Books, 2009.

Stone, Tanya Lee. *Amelia Earhart: A Photographic Story of a Life.* New York: Dorling Kindersley, 2007.

Websites

The Amelia Earhart Project
http://tighar.org/Projects/Earhart/AEdescr.html
Home page of an organization that searches for evidence that Amelia crash-landed on the island of Nikumaroro.

Centennial of Flight
www.centennialofflight.gov
A NASA online exhibit that discusses flight from 1903 through 2003.

The Dream of Flight
www.loc.gov/exhibits/treasures/wb-home.html
A Library of Congress online exhibit that chronicles the history of aviation.

George Palmer Putnam Collection of Amelia Earhart Papers
www.lib.purdue.edu/spcol/aearhart/
Papers and other artifacts donated to Purdue University by G. P. Putnam.

In Search of Amelia Earhart
www.museumofflight.org/amelia
The Museum of Flight's web page on the disappearance of Amelia.

The Ninety-Nines, Inc.
www.ninety-nines.org
Home page of the organization for women pilots that Amelia helped found.

Places to visit

Amelia Earhart Birthplace Museum
223 North Terrace Street
Atchison, KS 66002
913-367-4217
www.ameliaearhartmuseum.org

Amelia Earhart Earthwork
A portrait of Amelia carved into the ground by a Kansas artist.
17862 274th Road
Warnock Lake
Atchison, KS 66002
800-234-1854
www.travelks.com/s/index.cfm?LID=23

Dayton Aviation Heritage National Historic Park
16 South Williams Street
Dayton, OH 45402
937-225-7705
www.nps.gov/daav/index.htm

Smithsonian National Air and Space Museum
Independence Avenue Southwest
Washington, DC 20597
202-633-1000
www.nasm.si.edu

Index